Ankita Rossi

Elbe Radweg
(Elbe River Cycle Path)

Title: Elbe Radweg (Elbe River Cycle Path)
Author: Ankita Rossi
Published by: NEXTUNICORN PUBLISHER PROPRIETORSHIP
Publisher's Address: Shree Dwarkadhish Ji Ka Was, Emri, Rajsamand, RAJASTHAN, India. Pincode: 313342
Printer Details: Published online on various platforms.
Edition: 01
ISBN: 978-81-968464-4-2

Images Source: Pixbay: (https://pixabay.com/)
All images' rights belong to their respective owners.
Disclaimer: The author and publisher disclaim all liability for accuracy, loss, or damage arising from the use of this travel guide; users are urged to independently verify information and prioritize personal safety.

Catalog

Cultural Riches

Nestled along the picturesque Elbe River, the Elbe Radweg offers a tapestry of culture that is steeped in history and charm. While Paris may captivate with its allure, the enchanting cities of Dresden, Magdeburg, and Hamburg along the Elbe Radweg stand as a testament to a region that holds immense cultural significance. This area is not only a cradle of medieval history but also a hub of industrial innovation, providing an opportunity for profound exploration of its rich cultural heritage.

Dresden: Baroque Splendor on the Banks of the Elbe

Dresden, with its baroque splendor gracing the banks of the Elbe River, beckons you to discover architectural marvels such as the Frauenkirche and Zwinger Palace. The city's artistic legacy, from revered Old Masters to contemporary creators, comes alive within the walls of the Dresden State Art Collections.

Magdeburg: Where History Meets Modernity

Magdeburg seamlessly blends history with modernity and showcases landmarks like Magdeburg Cathedral and the Green Citadel. Take a leisurely stroll through its Old Town to witness an intriguing juxtaposition of medieval charm against contemporary vitality.

Hamburg: A Vibrant Port City

Hamburg is a bustling port city that offers an exciting blend of maritime history and vibrant culture. Explore historic Speicherstadt, marvel at HafenCity's modern architecture, and immerse yourself in the artistic energy emanating from Elbphilharmonie.

Off the Beaten Path

While the cities along Elbe Radweg shine brightly, there are hidden gems awaiting your discovery. Traverse charming villages adorned with half-timbered houses, explore medieval castles scattered along your route, and uncover artistic treasures tucked away in local galleries. The Elbe Radweg is more than just a cycling trail; it is a journey through time and culture.

Local Flair

Embrace the local way of life as you pedal along the Elbe Radweg. From the skilled craftsmanship of local artisans to the evolving culinary scene, each town and village has a unique story to tell. Discover the traditions of Elbe wine-making, indulge in regional specialties, and savor the warm hospitality of the communities along the Elbe River.

Gastronomic Delights

Similar to a meticulously set table, the Elbe Radweg offers a feast for your senses. From hearty local dishes to delectable pastries, every bite narrates a tale of culinary excellence. Relish in flavors sourced from regional produce, experience diverse gastronomic offerings in quaint cafes and gastropubs, and immerse yourself in the unique charm of Elbe-inspired cuisine.

Picturesque Landscapes

Beyond its cultural richness, the Elbe Radweg unveils breathtaking landscapes at every turn. Pedal through lush vineyards, follow the gentle curves of the tranquil Elbe River, and bask in nature's untouched reserves. Marvel at the beauty of the Elbe Sandstone Mountains and be captivated by serenity found along its winding path.

Outdoor Escapades

The Elbe Radweg promises not only a cultural journey but also outdoor adventures amidst nature's wonders. Whether cycling through scenic stretches of the Elbe Valley or hiking along picturesque trails, or engaging in water sports along its riverbanks, this route invites you to immerse yourself in diverse landscapes that grace this enchanting path.

Embark on an unforgettable adventure along the Elbe Radweg where each pedal stroke uncovers new facets of cultural heritage, gastronomic delights, and natural beauty. This cycling experience along one of Europe's most storied rivers is a celebration that embraces history, tradition while embodying vibrant spirit that defines these remarkable regions it traverses.

1. Dresden:

Dresden, famously known as the "Florence on the Elbe," has a captivating history that dates back to the 12th century. Despite being heavily damaged during World War II, this city has managed to rebuild itself and showcase its splendid baroque architecture.
When visiting Dresden, there are several key attractions worth exploring. One of them is the iconic Frauenkirche, which stands as a symbol of resilience. Additionally, art enthusiasts can indulge in the impressive art collections housed in Zwinger Palace.
To fully enjoy your visit, it's recommended to plan your trip during spring or summer when the weather is pleasant and adds to the city's allure.

If you're interested in visiting these attractions, here are their respective opening hours: Frauenkirche is open from 10 am to 6 pm from Monday to Saturday, while Zwinger Palace welcomes visitors from 6 am to 10 pm every day.

For any inquiries or further information about Frauenkirche and Zwinger Palace, you can contact them at +49 351 4846096 and +49 351 49142000 respectively.

While exploring Dresden, don't miss out on a hidden gem experience - a serene boat trip along the Elbe River. This unique perspective will allow you to appreciate Dresden's skyline in a whole new light.

Lastly, make sure to treat yourself with a culinary delight by trying Dresdner Stollen, a traditional Christmas fruitcake that will surely satisfy your taste buds.

2. Magdeburg:

Magdeburg, a city of captivating contrasts, seamlessly combines its rich history dating back to the 9th century with a vibrant modern atmosphere. Its unique blend of old-world charm and contemporary vibrancy makes it truly fascinating.

When exploring Magdeburg, be sure to visit the magnificent Magdeburg Cathedral, an architectural masterpiece showcasing stunning Gothic design. Another must-see attraction is the Green

Citadel, an architectural gem created by Friedensreich Hundertwasser.

For ideal weather conditions, plan your visit during spring or fall when temperatures are mild and perfect for outdoor exploration.

The opening hours for the Magdeburg Cathedral are from 10 am to 5 pm from Tuesday to Sunday. As for the Green Citadel, it welcomes visitors daily from 8 am to 8 pm.

If you need any further information or have inquiries about the Magdeburg Cathedral, you can reach them at +49 391 63601. For any questions regarding the Green Citadel, dial +49 391 744470.

One hidden gem in Magdeburg is the sprawling Elbauenpark. This expansive park offers a tranquil escape where you can relax and enjoy various recreational activities.

To truly indulge in local cuisine, make sure to try the mouthwatering specialty known as Magdeburger Halve Hahn.

3. Hamburg:

Hamburg, a city with a rich history dating back to the Middle Ages, has transformed into a bustling global port and a center of culture. There are some key attractions that you shouldn't miss when visiting Hamburg. Take some time to explore the historic Speicherstadt, which is known as the largest warehouse complex in the world. Another architectural marvel worth visiting is the Elbphilharmonie.

If you're wondering about the best time to visit Hamburg, consider going during the summer months. This is when you can experience vibrant harbor festivals and enjoy pleasant weather.

For those interested in planning their visit, it's important to note the opening hours of these attractions. The opening hours of Speicherstadt vary depending on the specific attraction you wish to visit. On the other hand, Elbphilharmonie opens its doors from 9 am until midnight every day.

In case you need to get in touch with these attractions for any reason, here are their contact numbers: +49 40 428131200 for Speicherstadt and +49 40 35766666 for Elbphilharmonie.

If you're looking for something off-the-beaten-path, I recommend exploring the Sternschanze district. This area is known for its eclectic boutiques and vibrant street art scene - a hidden gem waiting to be discovered.

No trip would be complete without trying some local culinary delights. Make sure to indulge in Fischbrötchen, a delicious fish sandwich that will surely satisfy your taste buds while immersing yourself in Hamburg's gastronomic offerings.

4. Meißen:

Let's delve into the captivating history of Meißen, a city that holds the prestigious title of being the birthplace of European porcelain. Its origins trace back to 929, making it a historical gem.

When you visit Meißen, make sure to immerse yourself in its key attractions. One such attraction is the magnificent Albrechtsburg Castle, which showcases remarkable medieval architecture. Another must-visit spot is the Meissen Porcelain Factory, where you can witness firsthand the intricate artistry behind European porcelain.

To truly experience Meißen's beauty, plan your visit during spring when nature comes alive with vibrant blooms. It's a time when the city flourishes with natural splendor.

If you're wondering about opening hours, take note that Albrechtsburg Castle welcomes visitors from 10 am to 5 pm from Tuesday to Sunday. As for the Meissen Porcelain Factory, it operates from 9 am to 6 pm every Monday through Saturday.

For any inquiries or further information, feel free to reach out to Albrechtsburg Castle at +49 3521 47070 or contact the Porcelain Factory at +49 3521 468208. They will be more than happy to assist you.

Beyond these well-known attractions lies a hidden gem waiting to be discovered - Meissen Cathedral's tranquil courtyard. Take some time to wander through its serene surroundings and soak in its peaceful ambiance.

And let's not forget about indulging in culinary delights while in Meißen! A must-try treat is Sächsische Eierschecke, a delectable regional layered cake that will tantalize your taste buds and leave you craving for more.

5. Torgau:

Torgau, a town with a rich history dating back to the Middle Ages, holds great significance during the Renaissance and the Protestant Reformation. It boasts several key attractions that are worth exploring, including the magnificent Torgau Castle, a true gem of Renaissance architecture, and the impressive Hartenfels Castle.

For those planning a visit, late spring is an ideal time to experience pleasant weather and witness the beauty of blooming landscapes. Be sure to take note of the opening hours: Torgau Castle welcomes visitors from 10 am to 5 pm (Tuesday to Sunday), while Hartenfels Castle is open from 10 am to 4 pm (Tuesday to Sunday).

If you have any inquiries or wish to contact these castles directly, you can reach out to them at +49 3421 758260 for Torgau Castle and +49 3421 758230 for Hartenfels Castle.

In addition to these well-known attractions, there's also a hidden gem waiting to be discovered in Torgau - the charming Kavalierhaus garden. This tranquil retreat offers a peaceful escape from bustling city life.

To truly immerse yourself in the local culture, don't miss out on indulging in Torgauer Doppelkekse, a delightful biscuit specialty unique to this area. It's sure to satisfy your taste buds with its distinct flavors.

6. Wittenberg:

Wittenberg has a fascinating history, as it was a significant place during the Reformation. It served as the residence of Martin Luther and was even the birthplace of the Protestant movement.

When you visit, be sure to explore the Luther House, where you can immerse yourself in history. Another must-visit attraction is the Castle Church, where Luther famously nailed his 95 Theses.

For the best experience, plan your trip during late spring or early autumn when temperatures are milder and there are fewer crowds.

The Luther House is open from 10 am to 6 pm from Tuesday to Sunday, while the Castle Church welcomes visitors from 9 am to 5 pm every day.

If you need to contact them, you can reach the Luther House at +49 3491 420757 and the Castle Church at +49 3491 401183.

One hidden gem in Wittenberg is taking a leisurely stroll along the Elbe River promenade. You'll be treated to stunning scenic views that will leave you in awe.

And don't forget to indulge in one of Wittenberg's culinary delights - try their local gingerbread specialty known as Wittenberger Lebkuchen. It's a true treat for your taste buds!

7. Dömitz:

Dömitz has a rich history, with its well-preserved medieval fortress standing as a testament to centuries of regional events and conflicts. One of the main attractions in Dömitz is the impressive military structure known as Dömitz Fortress, offering breathtaking panoramic views of the Elbe. The best time to visit is during the summer when you can take part in outdoor activities and enjoy various events. The fortress is open from 10 am to 6 pm, Tuesday through Sunday, and you can contact them at +49 5869 400. For a unique perspective, take a stroll along the medieval city walls, which are truly hidden gems waiting to be discovered. And when it comes to culinary delights, don't miss out on the opportunity to savor delicious regional fish dishes at the charming riverside restaurants in town.

8. Lauenburg:

Lauenburg, a town with its roots in the medieval era, has an enchanting old town and a fascinating history along the Elbe river. It offers a unique blend of perplexity and burstiness that sets it apart from other destinations.

When you visit Lauenburg, make sure to take a leisurely stroll through the old town and pay a visit to the historic Lauenburg Castle. The castle is open from 10 am to 5 pm, Tuesday through Sunday. For any inquiries or information about the castle, you can contact them at +49 4153 59090.

To fully appreciate the beauty of Lauenburg, it is recommended to visit during late spring or early autumn when the weather is pleasant and inviting. This will allow you to enjoy all that this charming town has to offer.

For those seeking hidden gems, don't miss out on exploring the Elbe bridge. It offers breathtaking panoramic views of the river that will leave you in awe of its natural beauty.

And when it comes to culinary delights, be sure to try Labskaus - a traditional sailor's dish made with corned beef and potatoes. It's an authentic taste of local cuisine that will satisfy your taste buds and leave you craving for more.

In conclusion, Lauenburg is more than just a historical destination; it's an experience filled with intrigue and wonder. So pack your bags and embark on an adventure like no other in this captivating town along the Elbe river.

9. Lutherstadt Eisleben:

Welcome to the historical town of Lutherstadt Eisleben! This charming place holds great significance as it is both the birth and deathplace of Martin Luther, a key figure in the Protestant Reformation. As you explore this town, you will come across several attractions that are worth visiting. The Luther Memorial is a must-see, where you can delve into the life and legacy of Martin

Luther. Don't forget to pay a visit to Luther's birthplace and his death house, which provide fascinating insights into his journey.

To make the most of your visit, it is recommended to plan your trip during late spring or early autumn when the temperatures are pleasant and comfortable. Keep in mind that the Luther Memorial operates from 10 am to 5 pm from Tuesday to Sunday.

For any inquiries or further information about the Luther Memorial, feel free to contact them at +49 3475 89830. Additionally, there's a hidden gem waiting for you in this town - Mansfeld Castle. Exploring this castle will give you even more historical insights and enrich your experience.

As you immerse yourself in the culture of Eisleben, don't miss out on trying one of their culinary delights - Eisleber Wiesenmarkt soup. This local festival specialty will tantalize your taste buds and leave you craving for more.

10. Schmilka:

Schmilka, a charming village in the Elbe Sandstone Mountains, is known for its peaceful ambiance and stunning natural scenery. When you visit this hidden gem, you'll have the opportunity to immerse yourself in the tranquility of the village and embark on exciting adventures along the nearby hiking trails. To make the most of your trip, consider visiting during spring or autumn when the weather is mild and the landscapes are adorned with vibrant colors. Don't miss out on exploring Schmilka's organic mill, where you can discover a wide range of regional products and even participate in workshops. And of course, indulging in locally-produced honey and organic cheeses is an absolute culinary delight that shouldn't be missed during your visit.

11. Riesa:

Riesa, a city with a rich history in craftsmanship and trade, is renowned for its porcelain production. As you take a leisurely walk along the Elbe River promenade, you'll be able to immerse yourself in the city's porcelain heritage. If you're planning a visit, summer is the perfect time as it offers pleasant temperatures and a chance to enjoy outdoor events. One hidden gem that shouldn't be missed is the Elbland Philharmonie, where you can experience captivating cultural performances. And of course, don't forget to indulge in Riesaer Sprotten, a local delicacy of smoked and salted herring that will surely satisfy your taste buds.

12. Dessau:

Dessau has a rich history in Bauhaus architecture, making it a significant contributor to the modernist movement. There are several key attractions in Dessau that you can explore, such as the Bauhaus Dessau Foundation and the UNESCO-listed Dessau-Wörlitz Garden Realm. If you're planning a visit, spring is a great time to see the blooming gardens, while autumn offers vibrant foliage. The Bauhaus Dessau Foundation is open from 10 am to 6 pm, Tuesday through Sunday. For any inquiries, you can contact them at +49 340 6508 101. Apart from these well-known spots, there's also a hidden gem called the Kornhaus Dessau, which was designed by Carl Fieger and is worth discovering. And when it comes to satisfying your taste buds, don't miss out on enjoying a meal at the Kornhaus Restaurant with its stunning view of the Elbe River.

Let's delve into the fascinating history of Cuxhaven, a charming coastal town with a vibrant maritime past. It has played a pivotal role as a bustling trading port throughout the ages.

When you visit Cuxhaven, be sure to immerse yourself in its captivating attractions. Take a leisurely stroll along the Alte Liebe pier and witness the breathtaking spectacle of the Elbe River merging with the vast expanse of the North Sea. It's truly a sight to behold!

If you're wondering about the best time to experience Cuxhaven's wonders, look no further than summer. This season offers an array of seaside activities and lively festivals that will keep you entertained and enthralled.

But here's a little secret gem that not many know about - make sure to pay a visit to the Kugelbake. This historic sea navigation aid holds countless stories within its walls, offering you an opportunity to step back in time and appreciate its significance.

And let's not forget about your taste buds! Indulge in the culinary delight that Cuxhaven has to offer by trying Finkenwerder Scholle, an exquisite local dish made from plaice. The flavors will transport you straight into seafood heaven!

Cuxhaven is truly a place where history meets natural beauty and delectable cuisine. So why wait? Start planning your trip now and embark on an unforgettable adventure in this coastal haven like no other!

14. Hitzacker:

Hitzacker, with its medieval old town, is a testament to its past as a bustling Hanseatic trading town. Strolling along the cobblestone streets, you can immerse yourself in the tranquility of the Elbe riverbanks. To fully enjoy the pleasant weather, it's best to visit in late spring or early autumn. One hidden gem of Hitzacker is the Hitzacker Music Festival, where you can experience captivating classical performances. And don't forget to treat yourself to a culinary delight by indulging in Hitzacker Marzipan, a delightful local sweet treat.

15. Tangermünde:

Tangermünde, with its beautifully preserved medieval architecture, is a true testament to its past as a Hanseatic city. Its history can be seen in every corner of the town.

When you visit Tangermünde, make sure to take in the breathtaking Town Hall and wander through the charming streets. The town has a unique charm that is hard to resist.

For the best experience, plan your visit to Tangermünde during late spring or summer. This is when you can enjoy outdoor events and festivals that showcase the vibrant spirit of the town.

One hidden gem that shouldn't be missed is Tangermünde Castle. It offers fascinating historical exhibitions that will transport you back in time.

And of course, don't forget to indulge in the local culinary delight - Tangermünder Torte. This almond cake is a true delicacy that will leave your taste buds wanting more.

Currency:
In Germany, as you travel along the Elbe Radweg, the official currency is the Euro (€). You'll find ATMs conveniently located in towns and cities, making it easy to access cash. When it comes to payment options, credit cards are widely accepted in hotels and restaurants, providing flexibility for travelers.
Language:
As you explore the Elbe Radweg, German is the official language. While English is commonly spoken in tourist areas, especially by younger people, learning a few basic German phrases can enhance your interactions with locals and enrich your travel experience.
Emergency Numbers:
In case of emergencies along the Elbe Radweg, keep these important contact numbers handy:
- Ambulance: 112
- Police: 110
- Fire: 112
If you need to make a call from outside Germany, remember to dial your international access code followed by Germany's country code (%49), and then the number (including the '0').
Useful Websites:
During your time on the Elbe Radweg, make use of these online resources:
- Elberadweg (www.elberadweg.de): The official website for information about the Elbe Radweg.
- Deutsche Bahn (www.bahn.de): The official website for train travel information in Germany.
- ADFC (www.adfc.de): The website of the German Cyclists' Association with cycling-related information.
- Slow Food Germany (www.slowfood.de): Discover local producers, markets, and culinary delights.
Daily Costs:
When it comes to daily expenses on the Elbe Radweg:

- Budget (Less than €100): You'll find affordable accommodation options and meals at local establishments.
- Midrange (€100–€250): Enjoy comfortable accommodations with reasonably priced meals and attractions.
- Top End (More than €250): Indulge in luxury accommodations and premium experiences along the Elbe Radweg.

Opening Hours:

Keep in mind that opening hours may vary depending on the season along the Elbe Radweg. Here are some general guidelines:
- Banks: Open from 9 am to 1 pm and 3 pm to 6 pm, Monday to Friday.
- Restaurants: Serving hours are typically from noon to 2:30 pm and 6:30 pm to 10 pm.
- Cafes: Open from 7 am to 8 pm.
- Shops: Most shops are open from 9 am to 1 pm and 3 pm to 7 pm, Monday to Saturday.

Arriving on Elbe Radweg:

Depending on where you start your journey along the Elbe Radweg, you may arrive at major airports or transportation hubs. Here are some key options:
- If you're arriving at Dresden Airport, you can make use of local transportation such as trains and buses to reach your starting point on the Elbe Radweg.

With this comprehensive guide, you're well-prepared for your exciting adventure on the Elbe Radweg. Get ready to immerse yourself in the cultural, historical, and natural wonders along this beautiful route.

Cultural Cycling along the Elbe - 2 Weeks

Embark on your Elbe Radweg journey in Dresden, a city known for its baroque splendor. Spend three days exploring the historic Frauenkirche, the art collections of Zwinger Palace, and the picturesque Elbe River.

As you cycle towards Magdeburg, immerse yourself in its historic charm and modern vibrancy. Take in landmarks such as Magdeburg Cathedral and the Green Citadel, experiencing the unique fusion of history and contemporary culture.

Continue your adventure in Wittenberg, where you can delve into Reformation history. Explore the Luther House and admire the town's medieval architecture, uncovering the roots of a significant historical period.

Next stop is Torgau, where you can step back into history at Torgau Castle. Marvel at the medieval architecture influenced by Renaissance aesthetics while enjoying the serene atmosphere and picturesque Elbe riverbanks.

Conclude your journey in Hamburg, a bustling port city. Immerse yourself in maritime history at Speicherstadt and revel in the contemporary culture showcased at Elbphilharmonie. Raise a glass to your cycling adventure along the Elbe Radweg.

Elbe Art and Architecture - 2 Weeks

Towns of Artistic Wonders:

Begin your exploration of artistic wonders along the Elbe Radweg with three days in Dresden. Admire its baroque splendor and visit renowned art collections that will leave you captivated.

Medieval Treasures:

Cycle to Meissen where European porcelain was born. Explore Albrechtsburg Castle and witness delicate craftsmanship at Meissen Porcelain Factory.

Renaissance Marvels:

Continue to Torgau to immerse yourself in Renaissance influences. Visit Torgau Castle and explore its medieval architecture that showcases an era of artistic brilliance.

Gothic Beauty:

Head to Magdeburg to experience its Gothic beauty. Take a leisurely stroll through the porticoed streets and savor the exquisite regional cuisine that will tantalize your taste buds.

Elbe Northwest Discovery - 2 Weeks

Art in Milan:

Commence your exploration of the northwest along the Elbe Radweg in Dresden. Marvel at artistic wonders in the city before embarking on your thrilling cycling adventure.

French-Influenced Turin:

Cycle to Magdeburg and hop on a train to Turin. Experience French-influenced architecture, historic cafes, and world-class museums that will transport you to a different time.

Wine in Alba:

Indulge in wine tasting in Alba as you continue your journey towards Genoa, famous for its pesto genovese that will leave you craving for more.

Coastal Hike:

End your exploration with a scenic hike along the stunning Cinque Terre coast. Marvel at terraced vines, picturesque villages, and indulge in delicious seafood that will satisfy both your eyes and taste buds.

Elbe Lakeside Serenity - 1 Week

Island Retreat in Dresden:

Start your lakeside serenity journey in Dresden. Explore the picturesque Elbe River and immerse yourself in the vibrant culture of this beautiful city.

Garden Exploration:

Cycle to Meissen and discover lakeside gardens where you can spend a leisurely day surrounded by natural beauty and tranquility.

Chic Bellagio:

Continue to Magdeburg and head towards chic Bellagio or explore Triangolo Lariano's mountainous hinterland for an unforgettable experience amidst breathtaking landscapes.

Romantic Lakeside Night:

Savor a final romantic night by the lakeside before concluding your serene lakeside retreat with memories that will last a lifetime.

Immersive Adventure in Enchanting Puglia - 2 Weeks

Romanesque Delights in Dresden:

Embark on your journey through Puglia with a visit to the captivating city of Dresden, renowned for its Romanesque cathedral. Take the time to soak in the city's unique charm before embarking on an exciting cycling adventure.

Exploring Valle d'Itria Towns:

Cycle through the picturesque towns of Valle d'Itria, including Alberobello, Locorotondo, Martina Franca, and Ostuni. Marvel at the region's rich history and architectural wonders as you pedal through charming landscapes.

Unwind at Blue-Flag Beaches in Otranto:

Indulge yourself in the beauty of Puglia's sandy blue-flag beaches in Otranto or Gallipoli. Immerse yourself in the coastal splendor and let your worries melt away.

Discovering the Southern Tip in Santa Maria di Leuca:

Conclude your unforgettable journey at Santa Maria di Leuca, located at the very tip of Italy's heel. Reflect on the diverse landscapes and cultural treasures that make Puglia truly special.

Captivating Elbe Expedition - 3 Weeks

Historical Marvels of Palermo:

Embark on an extraordinary expedition along the Elbe River starting from Dresden. Delight in exploring Palermo's historical treasures before setting off on your thrilling cycling adventure.

Diverse Landscapes of Sicily:

Pedal your way to Magdeburg and discover Sicily's diverse landscapes, from vibrant markets in Palermo to breathtaking mosaics at Cattedrale di Monreale.

Enchanting Aeolian Island Discovery:

Be amazed by the enchanting wonders of Aeolian Islands as you explore their unique landscapes and uncover hidden historical gems scattered throughout this spectacular region.
Immerse in Taormina's Vibrant Atmosphere:
Conclude your expedition in the vibrant town of Taormina, where you can relax on stunning beaches, hike the majestic Mt. Etna, and savor the diverse experiences Sicily has to offer.

Accommodation along the Elbe Radweg can be a delightful experience. To ensure a smooth and enjoyable stay, here are some helpful guidelines to keep in mind:

1. It's always a good idea to book your accommodations in advance, especially during peak cycling seasons or popular events in towns like Dresden and Magdeburg. This will help secure your preferred stay and avoid any last-minute hassles.

2. Keep in mind that accommodation prices can fluctuate with the seasons. During the summer months, you may encounter higher rates due to increased demand near the Elbe. However, if you plan your trip during quieter periods, you might find more budget-friendly options.

3. The location of your accommodation plays a significant role in determining its price. Rural towns often offer quaint guesthouses at more affordable rates compared to larger cities along the Elbe Radweg. So, consider regional variations when planning your cycling journey.

4. Some accommodations may provide meal packages as part of their offerings. It's worth checking if your chosen stay has options like half-board (breakfast and one other meal) or full board (all three meals). This can enhance your overall experience by ensuring you're well-fed during your adventure.

5. If you're traveling during the off-season, there might be room for negotiation when it comes to pricing, especially at smaller establishments. Don't hesitate to inquire about discounts or explore last-minute deals on platforms like Booking.com and local tourist offices for potential savings.

6. To secure your reservation, it's advisable to confirm with a credit card – particularly at smaller hotels along the Elbe Radweg. However, remember to familiarize yourself with their cancellation policies to avoid any charges for no-shows.

Now let's explore some of the accommodation options available along the Elbe Radweg:

1. Bed and Breakfasts (B&Bs): Immerse yourself in local hospitality by opting for charming B&Bs. These can range from restored farmhouses to city mansions, offering a unique and cozy stay. Prices per person typically vary from €30 to €100, providing budget-friendly options. For more information, you can visit Bed & Breakfast portals like [bbitalia.it](www.bbitalia.it).

2. Camping: If you prefer the outdoors, there are well-equipped campgrounds along the Elbe that offer a refreshing experience. Prices for campsites range from €10 to €25, with additional charges for adults and children. You can find a list of campgrounds on resources like [Campeggi.com](www.campeggi.com) and [Camping.it](www.camping.it).

3. Convents and Monasteries: For a unique accommodation experience, consider staying in convents and monasteries along the Elbe Radweg. Prices are generally reasonable, but do keep in mind that early curfews may apply. To explore your options further, visit websites like [MonasteryStays.com](www.monasterystays.com) and [In Italy Online](www.initaly.com).

4. Hostels: If affordability is key for you, hostels along the Elbe Radweg cater to diverse travelers with vibrant atmospheres. Dormitory beds typically range from €16 to €30 per night and often include breakfast. Check out associated youth hostels through Hostelling International (HI) for more details.

5. Hotels & Pensioni: Choose from a variety of hotels graded from one to five stars based on your preferences and budget along the Elbe Radweg. Prices vary depending on location, season, and quality of accommodations offered. Single rooms usually start from around €30 per night, while double rooms can range upwards from €50 per night or more.

6. Mountain Huts: For those seeking an alpine experience during their journey along the Elbe Radweg, staying in mountain huts can be a memorable choice. These huts operate seasonally and typically cost between €20 to €30 per person, including breakfast. Booking in advance is crucial, and the Club Alpino Italiano (CAI) operates many of these huts.

7. Rental Accommodation: If you prefer a more independent stay, renting apartments can provide flexibility during your trip. Short-term leases in major cities may cost around €1000 per month. Platforms like Guest in Italy, Homelidays, and Holiday Lettings offer various options for rental accommodations.

8. Villas: Indulge in scenic rural stays by renting villas along the Elbe Radweg. Prices for villas may vary depending on factors such as location and agency offering the properties. Agencies like Cuendet and Think Sicily are known for their beautiful villa options where you can experience comfort amidst picturesque surroundings.

Visas and Residency Along the Elbe Radweg

When it comes to planning a cycling journey along the Elbe Radweg, it's important to have a good understanding of the visa and residency regulations. This will ensure that your experience is smooth and compliant. Let's take a detailed look at the requirements for travelers:
1. Schengen Treaty for European Citizens:
   - If you're a European citizen from one of the countries that are part of the Schengen Treaty, you can start your adventure on the Elbe Radweg with a valid identity card or passport.
2. Visa Exemptions for Select Countries:
   - For citizens from non-EU countries, including but not limited to Australia, Brazil, Canada, Israel, Japan, New Zealand, and the USA, there might be visa exemptions for tourist visits of up to 90 days along the Elbe Radweg.
   - It's important to note that visa requirements may vary if you plan to travel beyond the Schengen zone.
3. Visas for Non-EU and Non-Schengen Nationals:
   - If you're a non-EU or non-Schengen national and you intend to cycle along the Elbe Radweg for more than 90 days or for purposes other than tourism (such as study or work), specific visas may be required.
   - You can find detailed and up-to-date information on visa requirements by visiting www.esteri.it/visti/home_eng.asp or contacting an Italian consulate.
4. Residence and Work for EU Citizens:
   - EU citizens who are cycling along the Elbe Radweg don't need permits to reside or work in Italy. However, if their stay exceeds three months continuously, they should register at their local municipal registry office and provide proof of work or sufficient financial means.
5. Permanent Residence for Non-EU Foreign Citizens:

- Non-EU foreign citizens who have completed five years of continuous legal residence in Italy may apply for permanent residence status.

6. Permesso di Soggiorno (Permit to Stay):

- Non-EU citizens planning to stay at a fixed address along the Elbe Radweg for more than one week should obtain a 'permesso di soggiorno' or permit to stay from the local police station.

- Tourists staying in hotels are usually exempt from this requirement.

- The 'permesso di soggiorno' becomes necessary for study, work, or extended residence and can be obtained from the police. The application process may take time and requires specific documents. For updated requirements, you can refer to www.poliziadistato.it under 'Foreign nationals.'

- EU citizens cycling along the Elbe Radweg generally do not need to obtain a 'permesso di soggiorno.'

7. Study Visas:

- Non-EU citizens planning to study at institutions along the Elbe Radweg must apply for a study visa at the nearest Italian embassy or consulate.

- Requirements typically include proof of enrollment, fee payment, and sufficient funds for the duration of studies.

- Study visas are issued based on the duration of enrollment and can be renewed within Italy with proof of ongoing studies and financial means.

By understanding these visa and residency details, you can ensure that your cycling journey along the Elbe Radweg is both legally compliant and enjoyable. Always check official sources for the latest requirements to make your travel plans easier. Have a safe adventure on your Elbe Radweg trip!

Detailed Route Descriptions for Elbe Radweg Cycling Adventure

Welcome to the detailed route descriptions for the Elbe Radweg cycling adventure! Whether you're a beginner or an experienced cyclist, this journey has something for everyone. Let's dive into the highlights and key information for each section of the route.

Section 1: From Schöneck to Asch

Start your adventure in Schöneck, a charming town surrounded by lush greenery. As you cycle through the serene Vogtland region, take in the beauty of rolling hills and picturesque villages. Don't miss out on visiting the Vogtland Arena, a renowned ski jumping venue that adds to the allure of this area.

The elevation profile for this section is moderate, with rolling hills and gradual ascents. It offers a great balance between challenge and enjoyment.

Section 2: From Asch to Dresden

Asch is famous for its historic architecture, including the Gothic Church of St. Nicholas. Traverse through the idyllic Ore Mountains that hold rich mining history. Your journey will lead you to Dresden, a cultural hub filled with iconic landmarks like Frauenkirche and Zwinger Palace.

In terms of elevation, this section presents varied terrain with moderate climbs. It's perfect for intermediate cyclists seeking a bit more challenge.

Section 3: Dresden to Torgau

Explore Dresden's baroque splendor as you visit iconic landmarks and art collections along your cycling route. Enjoy scenic views while pedaling along the beautiful Elbe River until you reach Torgau, known for its well-preserved medieval architecture.

The elevation profile here is mostly flat, with occasional gentle slopes that offer an easy ride suitable even for beginners.

Section 4: Torgau to Wittenberg

Discover the historical significance of Torgau Castle as you explore Renaissance influences in this charming town. Cycle through picturesque landscapes along the Elbe until you arrive in

Wittenberg, where Reformation history comes to life at the Luther House.

This section is mostly flat, with some gentle ascents that won't pose a challenge for beginners.

Section 5: Wittenberg to Dessau

Immerse yourself in Reformation history as you delve deeper into Wittenberg. Don't miss the opportunity to explore the UNESCO-listed Dessau-Wörlitz Garden Realm, renowned for its Bauhaus architecture. Enjoy cycling through the charming countryside along the Elbe, taking in the scenic beauty.

The elevation profile for this section is varied, with flat stretches and occasional gentle climbs. Intermediate cyclists will find it just right.

Section 6: Dessau to Magdeburg

Marvel at the impressive Bauhaus architecture in Dessau as you begin this leg of your journey. Cycle through the tranquil Elbe Sandstone Mountains and experience the serene atmosphere of Schmilka. Finally, arrive in Magdeburg, a city that seamlessly blends historic charm with modern vibrancy.

The elevation profile here offers a mix of challenges, with some demanding climbs interspersed among varied terrain. It's suitable for intermediate to advanced cyclists seeking an exhilarating experience.

Section 7: Magdeburg to Hamburg

Immerse yourself in Magdeburg's historic charm before embarking on a picturesque journey along the Elbe River towards Hamburg. Enjoy scenic riverbanks as you make your way towards this bustling port city that boasts maritime history and contemporary culture.

In terms of elevation, this section is mostly flat with some gentle slopes that won't pose difficulties even for beginners.

Section 8: Hamburg to Cuxhaven

Experience the maritime atmosphere of Hamburg before heading towards Cuxhaven, marking your final destination on the Elbe Radweg. Take in breathtaking coastal views and serene landscapes along your ride as you conclude your cycling adventure on a high note.

Key Junctions Along the Elbe Radweg

To navigate the Elbe Radweg with ease, it's helpful to have a guide that highlights the key junctions along the route. These junctions serve as important points of transition, showcasing notable landmarks and guiding cyclists on their scenic journey along the beautiful Elbe River. Let's take a closer look at some of these key junctions:

1. Schöneck Junction:
   - This is where your adventure on the Elbe Radweg begins.
   - From here, cyclists can connect to the picturesque Vogtland region.
   - Start your journey surrounded by stunning landscapes in Schöneck.

2. Asch Intersection:
   - Asch is renowned for its historic architecture, including the Church of St. Nicholas.
   - Cyclists transition from the Vogtland region to the Ore Mountains at this point.
   - On your way to Dresden, you'll encounter diverse terrains and breathtaking views.

3. Dresden Hub:
   - Dresden is a cultural gem along the Elbe Radweg.
   - Landmarks such as Frauenkirche, Zwinger Palace, and Semperoper await exploration.
   - Take in the baroque splendor and impressive art collections that this city has to offer.

4. Torgau Turnoff:
   - Torgau is a town known for its well-preserved medieval architecture.
   - Historical sites like Torgau Castle showcase Renaissance influences.
   - As cyclists continue their journey along the Elbe River, they'll enjoy flat terrains and scenic beauty.

5. Wittenberg Exchange:
   - Wittenberg holds significant importance in Reformation history.

- Landmarks like Luther House offer insights into this historical period.

   Transitioning towards Dessau will lead you through picturesque countryside scenery.

6. Dessau Intersection:

 + Dessau is recognized by UNESCO for its Dessau-Wörlitz Garden Realm and Bauhaus architecture.

 + Cyclists will experience diverse terrains, including the Elbe Sandstone Mountains.

 + Take a moment to appreciate the tranquility of Schmilka village.

7. Magdeburg Merge:

 - Magdeburg is a city that blends historic charm with modern vibrancy.

 - Key landmarks like Magdeburg Cathedral and the Green Citadel await exploration.

 - Cyclists will follow the Elbe River through mostly flat terrains, enjoying the beauty of their surroundings.

8. Hamburg Hub:

 - Hamburg is a bustling port city with a rich maritime history.

 - Explore attractions like Speicherstadt and the iconic Elbphilharmonie concert hall.

 - Immerse yourself in the lively atmosphere of Hamburg's riverbanks as you continue your cycling journey.

9. Cuxhaven Terminus:

 - Cuxhaven marks the endpoint of the Elbe Radweg.

 - Cyclists can soak in coastal views and enjoy the maritime ambiance of this charming town.

 - Your journey concludes in Cuxhaven, leaving you with lasting memories of your cycling adventure.

Understanding these key junctions will greatly assist cyclists in planning their route, discovering notable landmarks, and ensuring a seamless experience along the Elbe Radweg. May your journey be filled with stunning landscapes and unforgettable moments!

Schöneck Junction:
- If you're looking for a place to stay in Schöneck/Vogtland, Germany, you might consider Hotel Vogtland. Located at Bahnhofstraße 133, this hotel offers comfortable accommodations. You can reach them at +49 37464 33930. For more information, you can visit their website [here](https://hotelvogtland.com/).
- Another option in Schöneck/Vogtland is Hotel "Zur Talsperre". Situated at Tannenweg 3, this hotel offers a pleasant stay. You can contact them at +49 37464 3180. To learn more about the hotel, you can visit their website [here](https://www.hotel-schoeneck.de/).
Asch Intersection:
- If you're planning to visit Asch in the Czech Republic and need accommodation, consider Hotel Asch. Their address is Tyršova 225 and they can be reached at +420 354 454 111. For more details about the hotel, you can check out their website [here](https://www.hotel-as.cz/en/).
- Another option in Asch is Penzion U Johanky. Located at Karla Čapka 222, this guesthouse offers a cozy stay. You can contact them at +420 602 242 429. To find out more about Penzion U Johanky, please visit their website [here](https://www.penzionjohanka.cz/).
Dresden Hub:
- In Dresden, Germany, one of the recommended hotels is Hyperion Hotel Dresden am Schloss. Situated at Schloßstraße16, this hotel provides comfortable accommodations for your stay in Dresden. You can reach them at +49 35148460 or check out their website [here](https://www.h-hotels.com/de/hyperion/).
- Another option is Aparthotel Neumarkt, located at Neumarkt 9. They can be reached at +49 351484580. For more information about the aparthotel, you can visit their website [here](https://www.aparthotels-dresden.de/).
Torgau Turnoff:

- If you're passing through Torgau, Germany and need a place to stay, consider Hotel Torgauer Brauhof. Their address is Brauhof 7 and you can contact them at +49 3421 70100. To learn more about the hotel, visit their website [here](https://www.hotel-torgau.de/).
- Another option in Torgau is Hotel Goldener Anker, located at Markt 8. You can reach them at +49 3421 7250 or check out their website [here](https://www.goldener-anker-torgau.de/).
Wittenberg Exchange:
- Lutherstadt Wittenberg in Germany offers various accommodations for visitors. One of them is Luther-Hotel Wittenberg, situated at Neustraße 7-10. You can contact them at +49 3491 4980 or visit their website [here](https://www.luther-hotel-wittenberg.de/) for more details.
- Another option is Best Western soibelmanns Lutherstadt Wittenberg, located at Colonnaden29. They can be reached at +49 3491 4580. To find out more about the hotel, please visit their website [here](https://www.soibelmanns.com/).
Dessau Intersection:
  - If you're looking for a place to stay in Dessau-Roßlau, Germany, the Radisson Blu Fürst Leopold Hotel Dessau is an excellent choice. You can find it at Friedrichstraße 151. Feel free to give them a call at +49 340 25120 or visit their website [here](https://www.radissonhotels.com/en-us/hotels/radisson-blu-dessau).
  - Another option in Dessau-Roßlau is NH Dessau located at Zerbster Str. 29. To make reservations or gather more information, you can contact them directly at +49 340 25640. Their website is [NH Dessau](https://www.nh-hotels.com/hotel/nh-dessau).
Magdeburg Merge:
  - For those heading to Magdeburg, Germany, the Maritim Hotel Magdeburg on Otto-von-Guericke-Straße 87 offers a comfortable stay. Contact them at +49 391 59490 or visit their website [here](https://www.maritim.com/en/hotels/germany/hotel-magdeburg).
  - Alternatively, you can consider the Dormero Hotel Magdeburg situated at Leipziger Chaussee 141. Get in touch with them

directly at +49 391 288860 or check out their website
[here](https://www.dormero.de/en/hotel-magdeburg/).
Hamburg Hub:
   - In Hamburg, Germany, The Westin Hamburg located on Platz
der Deutschen Einheit 2 is an excellent choice for accommodation.
You can reach them at +49 40 800010 or visit their website
[here](https://www.marriott.com/hotels/travel/hamwi-the-
westin-hamburg/).
   - Another option is the Reichshof Hamburg, Curio Collection by
Hilton situated at Kirchenallee 34-36. Feel free to contact them at
+49 40 3702590 or visit their website
[here](https://www.reichshof-hamburg.de/en/).
Cuxhaven Terminus:
   - Hotel Strandhus on Cuxhavener Straße 86 in Cuxhaven,
Germany, offers a pleasant stay for travelers. Give them a call at
+49 4721 39900 or visit their website [here](https://www.hotel-
strandhus.de/) for more information.
   - Alternatively, you can consider Moin Hotel Cuxhaven located
at Cuxhavener Straße 156. Contact them directly at +49 4721
50890 or check out their website [here](https://www.moinhotel-
cuxhaven.de/en/).
These hotels provide various accommodation options to ensure a
comfortable stay for cyclists exploring the Elbe Radweg. For the
latest information and reservations, it's best to visit the respective
hotel websites or contact them directly.

Komoot stands out as an exceptional option for cyclists exploring the Elbe Radweg. It offers comprehensive route planning with detailed elevation profiles and highlights of key attractions along the way. What's more, the app even works offline, ensuring seamless navigation in areas with no cellular signal. Cyclists can also track their rides, share experiences, and discover recommended routes from fellow cyclists.

Another popular choice among cyclists is Strava. This app boasts robust navigation features that allow users to plan routes, track their rides, and analyze their performance. The global community on Strava provides valuable insights into popular routes and cycling trends. With its real-time segment tracking feature, it adds a competitive element to the ride that appeals to those seeking challenges.

For a versatile navigation experience, Google Maps is an excellent option for cyclists on the Elbe Radweg. It offers accurate turn-by-turn directions, real-time traffic updates, and information about nearby amenities. Cyclists can plan custom routes, save offline maps for offline use, and explore points of interest along the beautiful Elbe River. Google Maps is widely used and seamlessly integrates with other Google services.

Catering specifically to cyclists' needs is Bikemap - an app designed with a user-friendly interface for planning and navigating bike routes. It boasts a large community of cyclists who share their favorite routes and recommendations. Offline maps are available for uninterrupted exploration along with important details such as elevation profiles and surface types - crucial factors for cyclists on the Elbe Radweg.

OsmAnd takes pride in being a comprehensive offline map and navigation app based on OpenStreetMap data - perfect for cyclists venturing into areas with limited connectivity. It offers detailed maps, turn-by-turn navigation guidance, and customizable route planning options tailored to meet specific cycling requirements.

Additionally, OsmAnd provides valuable information about points of interest as well as elevation profiles.

MapOut is another intuitive mapping app that allows cyclists to effortlessly plan and navigate routes. Its offline map feature makes it a reliable companion for remote sections of the Elbe Radweg. With customization options for route planning and the ability to download maps for offline use, MapOut provides a practical solution for cyclists. Its simple interface and focus on offline functionality make it an excellent choice.

Runtastic Road Bike GPS, which is part of the Adidas Running app, caters specifically to cyclists' needs. It offers route tracking, live tracking, and performance analysis features. Cyclists can access elevation data, integrate with wearables, and set fitness goals within the app. Moreover, they can discover routes shared by the community and receive voice coaching during their rides.

Lastly, Locus Map is a versatile navigation app suitable for cyclists exploring the Elbe Radweg. It offers offline maps along with route planning and navigation capabilities. The app supports various map sources including OpenStreetMap. Cyclists can record their rides, analyze their performance, explore points of interest along the way, and take advantage of advanced navigation tools provided by Locus Map.

These mobile navigation apps cater perfectly to the needs of cyclists on the Elbe Radweg by providing essential features such as route planning options, offline maps for uninterrupted exploration even in areas with no cellular signal coverage, as well as real-time tracking capabilities. Cyclists have a wide range of choices available to them based on their preferences and specific navigation requirements when exploring this beautiful cycling route.

When it comes to exploring the Elbe Radweg, the local tourist information centers play a vital role in assisting cyclists and providing them with valuable insights, maps, and guidance about the region. Let me introduce you to some of the key tourist information centers along the Elbe Radweg:

1. Dresden Tourist Information Center:
   - Location: QF Passage, Neumarkt 2, 01067 Dresden, Germany
   - Contact: +49 351 50173000
   - Website: [Dresden Tourist Information Center](https://www.dresden.de/en/tourism/tourist-information/tourist-information.php)
   - Services: At this center, you can gather detailed information about Dresden, pick up maps, and receive assistance in planning your journey along the Elbe Radweg.

2. Magdeburg Tourist Information:
   - Location: Breiter Weg 22, 39104 Magdeburg, Germany
   - Contact: +49 391 19433
   - Website: [Magdeburg Tourist Information](https://www.magdeburg-tourist.de/en/)
   - Services: The tourist center in Magdeburg offers information about local attractions and accommodations. They can also provide guidance specifically for cyclists embarking on the Elbe Radweg.

3. Hamburg Tourismus:
   - Location: Wexstraße 7, 20355 Hamburg, Germany
   - Contact: +49 40 30051300
   - Website: [Hamburg Tourismus](https://www.hamburg-travel.com/)
   - Services: If you're visiting Hamburg and planning to explore the Elbe Radweg by bike, Hamburg Tourismus is your go-to resource. They provide comprehensive information about the city as well as maps and resources for cyclists.

4. Lutherstadt Wittenberg Tourist Information:

- Location: Schlossplatz 2, 06886 Lutherstadt Wittenberg, Germany
  - Contact: +49 3491 498610
  - Website: [Lutherstadt Wittenberg Tourist Information](https://www.wittenberg.de/en/tourism/tourist-information.html)
  - Services: Discover the historical significance of Wittenberg at this tourist information center. They can provide you with cycling information and guide you to key attractions along the Elbe Radweg.
5. Dömitz Tourist Information:
  - Location: An der Festung 3, 19303 Dömitz, Germany
  - Contact: +49 3863 2140
  - Website: [Dömitz Tourist Information](https://www.doemitz.de/tourismus/)
  - Services: If you're passing through the Elbe region, make sure to visit Dömitz Tourist Information. They offer insights into the medieval fortress and provide resources specifically for cyclists exploring the Elbe Radweg.
6. Lauenburg Tourist Information:
  - Location: Elbstraße 145, 21481 Lauenburg, Germany
  - Contact: +49 4153 59090
  - Website: [Lauenburg Tourist Information](https://www.lauenburg-tourismus.de/en/)
  - Services: Immerse yourself in the charm of Lauenburg's old town and seek assistance from this tourist information center. They can provide you with valuable information and maps for your journey along the Elbe Radweg.
7. Tangermünde Tourist Information:
  Location: Lange Straße 52, 39590 Tangermünde, Germany
  Telephone: +49 39322 788780
  Website: [Tangermünde Tourist Information](https://www.tangermuende-tourismus.de/en/)
  Services: Marvel at the medieval architecture of Tangermünde and gather all the resources you need for your exciting journey along the Elbe.

Remember, these tourist information centers are there to make your cycling experience along the Elbe Radweg more enjoyable and hassle-free. So be sure to stop by and take advantage of their services!